Ashridge Estate

HERTFORDSHIRE

A souvenir guide

CW00765873

THE NATIONAL TRUST

INTRODUCING ASHRIDGE

The Ashridge Estate lies only thirty miles from central London and close to large towns like Hemel Hempstead and Aylesbury. Yet this elevated landscape, with its open chalk hills and majestic beech woods, feels wonderfully remote.

Visitors may think this is countryside in all its natural glory, unsullied by the activities of man, but it is not. The landscape looks the way that it does because it has been used in particular ways over very many centuries – and because it is managed in particular ways today. Nevertheless, nature provided the bones of the countryside – the shapes of hills and valleys – and the raw materials from which successive generations fashioned this distinctive place.

Rocks of ages

Ashridge lies high in the Chilterns, a range of hills which runs in a line, orientated roughly north-east to south-west, a little way to the north of London. The hills are composed of chalk, a white porous limestone formed from the remains of billions of tiny creatures that lived in a warm sea around a hundred million years ago. They represent the northern edge of a great trough or basin of sediments, in the central and lowest part of which lies London and the River Thames; the southern edge of the trough is formed by the North Downs. Hard, dark, irregular nodules of flint occur in marked bands within the chalk, the consequence of chemical action in the remote past. The hills have a steep slope, or escarpment, to the north-west, overlooking the lower ground of the Vale of Aylesbury. To the south, however, the slope falls almost imperceptibly towards London, but it is cut by a number of sharp valleys, some now dry, which were formed by watercourses running at right angles to the escarpment. As a result, the Chilterns consist of a fairly level upland plateau which is interrupted at intervals by steep slopes. The chalk is exposed on these slopes – on the escarpment itself, and on the sides of the larger valleys – and gives rise to light, freely draining soils. Elsewhere it is covered by 'clay-with-flints', a fairly permeable, rather acidic clay containing large numbers of flint pebbles.

The lie of the land

These two formations, and the soils which derive from them, give rise to very different kinds of landscape on the Ashridge Estate. A long tongue of estate land extends northwards, onto the steep chalk slopes of the escarpment, and in the area around Ivinghoe Beacon (1) and Incombe Hole (2) there are wide expanses of open chalk grassland. The bulk of the estate, however, lies on the clay-with-flints plateau, and the landscape here has been occupied for the larger part of the last millennium by woods and commons. This is a general distinction, however, and not a hard and fast one; in places the woods spill from the plateau down some of the steeper slopes, most dramatically below the Bridgewater Monument (6), towards the picturesque village of Aldbury.

Opposite The plateau consists of woodland and commons, with many ancient beech trees

AN ANCIENT LANDSCAPE

Ashridge is rich in archaeological traces of prehistoric and Roman settlement. Such remains are particularly obvious in the form of earthworks in the open chalk grassland to the north of the estate.

These earthworks include numerous ancient field boundaries; groups of burial mounds or barrows dating from the Bronze Age; and substantial linear boundaries from the Iron Age, which form part of an extensive system running all along the Chilterns, and to which the name 'Grims Ditch' has traditionally been given. Most striking of all is the great enclosure or hillfort of Ivinghoe Beacon, built at the end of the Bronze Age, around 700 BC. In addition, there are also many stretches of droving routes surviving as depressions or parallel lines of bank and ditch, which run both along and across the escarpment. The former are thought to be part of the long-distance prehistoric route called the Icknield Way, which extended all the way from East Anglia to Wessex.

First farmers

Together, this collection of ancient earthworks forms a landscape of national importance. Its presence here reflects the fact that prehistoric farmers found it easier to cultivate the light, freely draining soils of the chalk than the

Below Ivinghoe Hills seen from the air show evidence of Bronze Age earthworks and Iron Age fortification

The oldest road in Britain

The Icknield Way is one of four long-distance footpaths which, when combined, run from Lyme Regis in Dorset to Hunstanton in Norfolk and are referred to as the Greater Ridgeway. Perhaps deriving its name from the Iceni tribe who occupied present-day Norfolk, it was established before the arrival of the Romans. A modern footpath, known as the Icknield Way Path, extends from Ivinghoe Beacon here at Ashridge to Knettishall Heath in Norfolk, and follows in the footsteps of the ancient Britons. Prehistoric droving routes (see opposite) dotted with archaeological remains now survive as splendid tracks and green lanes along the chalk 'spine' of England.

heavier soils found in the vale north of the escarpment, or those derived from the acid clay-with-flints on the plateau to the south.

However, by late prehistoric times there is little doubt that fields and farms also existed on the heavier soils of the vale, but no clear signs of these remain. In addition, although evidence for early settlement is most obvious in the open landscape of the chalk grasslands, subtler signs indicate that the wooded plateau of the estate was being opened up for farming and settlement by the late Iron Age – a time when the population appears to have been rapidly growing throughout Britain, and all kinds of difficult and marginal land were being settled and cultivated.

Careful archaeological survey by the National Trust has revealed traces of farms, lanes and fields of Iron Age and Roman date buried within the Ashridge woods, surviving as networks of low banks, or indicated by concentrations of pottery fragments found on the surface. Clearly, some parts of the plateau were being settled and farmed, but the extensive tracts of woodland also seem to have survived. Many of these settlements have produced evidence of slag, a by-product of smelting iron ore – probably so-called 'bog iron', which occurs naturally in the valley of the river Bulbourne a few kilometres to the south-west. Smelting required large amounts of fuel, most probably cut from the surrounding woodlands.

The marks left on Ashridge's landscape by people through the successive periods of history tell an intriguing story but not always a complete one. For instance, the concentrations of early earthworks in the chalk glasslands to the north indicating prehistoric settlement also mark an area which later people, in the Middle Ages and after, found hard or uneconomic to cultivate. If the land had been ploughed for any length of time, even the largest of these would have been levelled.

Below These sunken ways over Ivinghoe Beacon are the result of millennia of droving

ASHRIDGE IN THE MIDDLE AGES

In the period following the end of Roman rule in Britain, the population declined and the farms and fields on the high ground around Ashridge seem to have been abandoned. But this does not mean that the area was an unused wilderness, and soon after the Norman Conquest nobles and monks began to make a permanent mark on this wooded landscape.

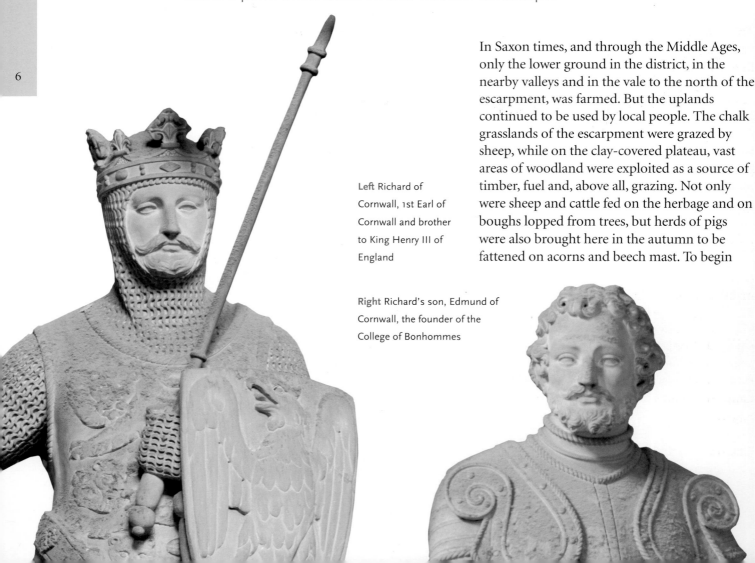

Left Richard of Cornwall, 1st Earl of Cornwall and brother to King Henry III of England

Right Richard's son, Edmund of Cornwall, the founder of the College of Bonhommes

In Saxon times, and through the Middle Ages, only the lower ground in the district, in the nearby valleys and in the vale to the north of the escarpment, was farmed. But the uplands continued to be used by local people. The chalk grasslands of the escarpment were grazed by sheep, while on the clay-covered plateau, vast areas of woodland were exploited as a source of timber, fuel and, above all, grazing. Not only were sheep and cattle fed on the herbage and on boughs lopped from trees, but herds of pigs were also brought here in the autumn to be fattened on acorns and beech mast. To begin with, large tracts seem to have been shared or 'intercommoned' between different communities. As late as 1363 the 309-hectare (763-acre) wood called The Frith was used by people living in Berkhamsted, Northchurch, Nettleden and Gaddesden, and even by those living as far away as Bovingdon and Flaunden, and in Pitstone and Chevington to the north of the escarpment.

Enclosing the park

This wild and wooded landscape also provided opportunities for farming venison and hunting deer, and some time in the 13th century 80 hectares (200 acres) at Ashridge were enclosed as a park. This was probably done around 1265 by Richard, Earl of Cornwall, who held nearby Berkhamsted Castle. The boundary pale – a bank originally topped with a wooden fence – can still be traced in many places. The park, like most examples, contained a lodge to provide accommodation for the park-keeper and for the owner while on hunting trips. That at Ashridge must have been a substantial building, as Richard's son Edmund allegedly made it his favourite residence, neglecting to properly maintain the castle at Berkhamsted.

The monastery

Edmund also founded a small monastery here in around 1283. It was occupied by the Bonhommes, an Augustinian Order of Canons. The order was also known as the Bluefriars on account of the monks' coloured robes. The monastery's endowments included a phial of Christ's blood, guaranteed as genuine by no less than the Patriarch of Jerusalem. The monastery was not large – there were never more than 20 monks – but it had a respectable range of buildings, including a church, hall and refectory arranged round a central cloister. It stood on the site now occupied by Ashridge House (9), and the remains of one of its undercrofts, or cellars, still survive beneath part of the present building. The upland woods provided a suitably secluded dwelling for the monks, but while Ashridge was remote from other settlements, the monastery and lodge were on a well-beaten track. Edward I, Edmund's cousin, held a parliament here in 1290. As important a place as it had once occupied, the monastery did not escape the Reformation and in 1539 was dissolved with each monk receiving a pension for life.

Below The monastic buildings survived, much altered, into the 18th century

Above The Bridgewater
Monument, designed by
Sir Jeffry Wyatville and
erected in 1832 to
commemorate the
achievements of the
Canal Duke

THE OWNERS OF ASHRIDGE

Ashridge passed out of the hands of monks and became the centre of a great
landed estate. The monastery became a mansion set in elaborate grounds,
while the farms and fields for many miles around were the private property of a
succession of wealthy individuals.

Following the Dissolution, the monastery and
its surrounding lands became the property of
the Crown, and in 1550 were conveyed by
Edward VI to his sister Elizabeth. At that time
the estate included some 300 acres of woodland
and 300 acres of farmland, together with
stables, barns, dovecotes, orchards and gardens.
Elizabeth spent much time here before she
became queen, so much time in fact it became
a virtual prison for the young princess, so when
the opportunity came in 1575, she sold the
property. It passed through several hands
before it was acquired in 1604 by Sir Thomas
Egerton, Lord Chancellor and Baron Ellesmere,
whose son became the 1st Earl of Bridgewater.

The Canal Duke
The family prospered and in 1720 Scroop
Egerton (1681–1744) was created the 1st Duke of
Bridgewater. His son Francis (1736–1803), who
became the 3rd Duke after the death of Francis's
elder brother aged only 20, is renowned as the
'Canal Duke'. He employed the engineer James
Brindley to construct the Bridgewater Canal –
arguably the first true canal in England – to
service his coal mines at Worsley in Lancashire.
Some years after his death the second architect
of Ashridge, Sir Jeffry Wyatville, was
commissioned under the terms of the will of the

8th and last Earl of Bridgewater to design the
Bridgewater Monument (6) to celebrate his
ancestor's achievements. This soaring Grecian
column, topped with an urn, was erected in 1832
and stands to this day. Indeed, visitors may
climb to the top to enjoy the magnificent views.

The Brownlows

The Canal Duke did not marry and had no children, and so on his death the estate, but not the dukedom, passed to his first cousin once removed, the soldier and politician John William Egerton (1753–1823), who became 7th Earl of Bridgewater. He died without offspring and was succeeded by his younger brother Francis (1756–1829). Francis died six years later, also without progeny, and the Bridgewater title died with him. The estate passed to Francis's great-nephew, John Hume Egerton, Viscount Alford (1812–51). When he died, the battle that ensued over his will became one of the most famous legal cases of the 19th century – 'Egerton vs Brownlow'. The Brownlows triumphed and in 1853 John Hume was succeeded by his son John William, who also inherited the title of 2nd Earl Brownlow from his father. In addition to Ashridge and the earldom, John William inherited the Brownlow estates at Belton in Lincolnshire (also National Trust).

9

Brownlow earls continued to own Ashridge until the 1920s. Yet for much of the 19th century the estate was effectively run by women: between 1823 and 1849 by the 7th Earl of Bridgewater's widow, Charlotte Catherine; and in the middle decades of the century by Marian Alford, after the premature death of John Hume Cust in 1851, until her son John Willam, the 2nd Earl Brownlow, came of age in 1863.

Agriculture did well for most of the late 18th and 19th centuries, but the estate's owners also made money from industrial rents and investments. The Canal Duke in particular did well from his mines and other industrial enterprises, and had an annual income of around £80,000 – a vast sum for the day. Such profits were used to buy more land, and by 1871 the estate extended over some 8,900 hectares (22,000 acres) in Hertfordshire, Bedfordshire and Buckinghamshire.

Below The 2nd Earl Brownlow by Sir Francis Grant. The Brownlow Collection located at Belton

Left Lady Marian Alford by Sir Francis Grant. The Brownlow Collection located at Belton

ASHRIDGE HOUSE AND PARK

Like other great estates, Ashridge comprised farms, fields, woods and cottages, but at its heart lay the mansion with its park and gardens. Ashridge House and its gardens were never acquired by the National Trust, but the mansion nevertheless forms the focal point of the designed landscape that the Trust today maintains.

The original monastic buildings, added to and altered over the years, survived until the 1760s when the Canal Duke commissioned the architect Henry Holland to design a new house, slightly to the east. But the present Ashridge House (9) is essentially a creation of John William Egerton who, immediately after he inherited the estate in 1803, commissioned the architect James Wyatt to design him a vast new home. This was in the fashionable Gothic style – inspired by the architecture of the Middle Ages, in contrast to the prevailing classical models employed for country houses during the previous century. Wyatt died before the work was completed and the task of finishing the design fell to his nephew Jeffry, another Gothic-influenced architect, who even changed his name to Wyatville because it sounded more medieval. He made many alterations to his uncle's design, creating a house that was larger, less symmetrical and in general more dramatic and romantic. The result is a dizzying collection of battlements and turrets, dominated by a great abbey tower. It boasts the longest frontage of any house in England – around 300 metres. Its style seems perfectly suited to this wild, high, wooded landscape, once the playground of royalty.

Below Engraving of the north front of Ashridge, from H.J. Todd's *History of the College of Bonhommes at Ashridge*, 1823

Park invaders

The house was raided on a number of occasions by Royalist troops during the Civil War, and in 1643 the first Earl of Bridgewater complained that they had ransacked the house and park, killing 'not only male deers but does ready to fawn, and fawns that could hardly stand'.

The formal park

The park and gardens surrounding the mansion went though many complex changes over the centuries. The deer park created by Richard Earl of Cornwall had been reduced in size to a mere 34 hectares (83 acres) by 1575, but shortly after 1660 the 2nd Earl of Bridgewater enclosed 62 hectares (400 acres) of common woodland to the north and west of the house and formed the Old Park (11). Accommodation was provided for the park keeper – the building now known as Old Park Lodge. The rights of the commoners were extinguished and a number of public roads were closed. By this time, parks were designed landscapes, intended to provide a magnificent setting for a mansion, rather than simply deer farms and hunting grounds.

The prevailing fashion was for very formal, geometric gardens and parks, and at Ashridge the house and its walled gardens (which included a 'mount' or viewing mound which still survives to the south of the house) were framed to the south-west by a wide avenue planted with elm and lime trees, while to the north broad, straight rides or 'ridings' were cut through the woodland, focused on the mansion: the Princes Riding (7), lined with beech, and the Ash Riding, lined, unsurprisingly, with ash. The Princes Riding is still a prominent feature of the landscape, although none of its original trees survives. It now leads to the Bridgewater Monument (6), from the top of which the house can be glimpsed, framed by the trees, two and a half kilometres away.

Top Old Park Lodge, drawn in 1805 by Henry Edridge (1769–1821)

Above Sir Jeffry Wyatville (1766–1811), drawn in 1855 by Sir Francis Leggatt Chantrey (1781–1841)

Above The Holie Well from Repton's 'Red Book'

THE DESIGNERS OF ASHRIDGE

The 18th century

In the middle decades of the 18th century a new, more naturalistic style of landscape design became fashionable, under the influence of designers like Lancelot 'Capability' Brown. Avenues, straight lines and geometric planting, as well as walled gardens, fell from favour. The fashion was now for extensive panoramas of turf, scattered in a casual, naturalistic fashion with individual trees and clumps. Gardens were normally marginalised from the main view, so that the house appeared to stand in open parkland. Brown himself worked at Ashridge in the 1760s, at the same time as his friend Henry Holland was building a new house for the Earl. Although many of the old formal elements of the landscape were allowed to remain, Brown softened the lines of planting immediately to the north-west of the house, removing trees to open up lawns and vistas, and to create a number of large oval clumps. His greatest work, however, was to the north-east of the mansion. Here the Golden Valley (8) was made by removing trees along the base and sides of a narrow, dry valley, leaving woodland with sinuous edges on either side. Originally, gaps were left in the planting along the southern side of the valley so as to allow distant glimpses of the mansion. It remains one of Brown's finest works.

Above left Lancelot 'Capability' Brown (1716–83) by Nathaniel Dance

Left Humphry Repton (1752–1818)

The 19th century

There were further changes to the landscape when the new Gothic mansion was erected in the early 19th century, this time the work of another famous designer – Humphry Repton. This was a period when gardens were beginning to come back into fashion as the main setting for great houses. In 1813 Repton drew up a 'Red Book' for the grounds. This was a set of design proposals, bound in red leather and illustrated with watercolours, many of which featured Repton's trademark device – a lift-off flap showing the results of the suggested alterations. He proposed an elaborate series of gardens, many of which harked back to the geometric designs of the past and otherwise made references to the site's medieval history and the Gothic style of the house itself. They thus included a 'Monk's Garden' and a 'Holie Well'. Many, but not all, of his ideas were executed under the direction of Wyatville. The gardens were further developed during the 1850s and 60s, largely under the direction of Marian, Viscountess Alford. An armorial garden was created in which the arms of the families associated with the estate – Brownlow, Egerton, Cust and Compton (Lady Marian's own family) – were laid out in box hedging. Most impressive of all, an extensive Italian Garden, featuring a central raised pond, clipped yews and box parterres planted with bedding plants, was created immediately to the south of the house. Both have recently been restored by Ashridge Business School, which now owns the house.

Opposite Golden Valley

The designed intent

The rather wild and romantic appearance of the 19th-century park appealed to the contemporary taste for the picturesque. The great garden designer John Claudius Loudon (1783–1843) described it as follows: 'Every variety of effect is produced that can result from a variety of disposition of trees and groups; thickets, scattered trees and bushes, ferns, furze, hollies, thorns, glades, recesses and natural vistas, succeed each other in endless variety.'

FARMS, FIELDS AND COTTAGES

The great estate

The great Gothic pile of Ashridge House (9), secluded within its park, lay at the heart of the estate, and – rather unusually for a large landed property – was mainly ringed by commons and woodland. The areas of productive farmland, the rents from which were one of the main sources of revenue, lay further afield. The original Ashridge Estate covered much more ground than the National Trust currently owns and manages, extending well beyond the woods and pastures of the plateau. To the south, it included fields and farms in the valley of the river Bulbourne, as well as property in the town of Berkhamsted including the castle; to the north-east it embraced most of the cultivated land in Great and Little Gaddesden, as well as the majority of the houses there; while to the east the bulk of the parish of Aldbury was included within it. But the main area of the estate lay to the north-west, in the vale below the escarpment, where almost all of the land, and most of the houses, in the villages of Pitstone, Edlesborough, Ivinghoe, Ivinghoe Aston, Slapton, Horton and Cublington eventually became estate property. By the 19th century the majority of the people living across an extensive area at the junction of Hertfordshire, Buckinghamshire and Bedfordshire worked for the estate, or on farms owned by the estate.

Above Thunderdell Lodge

A little 'kingdom'

Great estates were obliged to keep the farms, houses and agricultural buildings of their tenants in good repair, but in the course of the 19th century they also took an increasing interest in the housing of the estate labourers and farmworkers. Under Lady Marian Alford and the 2nd and 3rd Earls Brownlow, many of the old houses on the estate, especially in the area around the mansion, were improved, and new ones erected. But great landowners delighted in showing the extent of their possession, and many of the houses around Ashridge were painted the same plum colour,

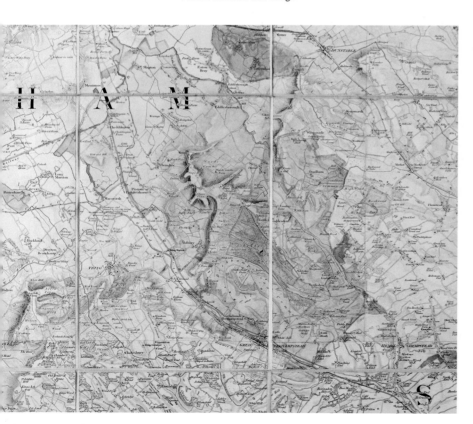

Left Map dated 1853 showing the estate approaching its greatest extent

Lords of all whom they survey

The owners of Ashridge took an active interest in the affairs of the local communities, an interest which was both benevolent and intrusive. As well as building schools and almshouses, they dominated the parish churches (usually appointing the parson) and laid down strict rules for their tenants. Leases for cottages included such clauses as 'Every room to be lime washed once a year, in May, at the expense of the tenant, the landlord delivering lime on the premises' and 'The bedroom windows, unless in the case of illness, to be opened every morning from 8 o'clock until 12 o'clock'. Feudalism no longer operated but the idea of the feudal lord certainly lived on. That said, these 'lords' provided employment to a great many people in the local area.

Above A house on the estate bearing the Brownlow coat of arms

and numbered with small blue-and-white tiles. In other ways the estate buildings were made more acceptable to polite taste: many were given a fashionable makeover, sometimes more than one, in the 19th century. Home Farm, for example, was provided with Tudor gables in 1841, and improved more comprehensively in 1877 when it was given a 'skin' of bricks, new doors and windows. Like many of the former estate buildings it still carries the crest of the Brownlow family. Although the estate's owners exercised tight control over an extensive tract of countryside, it was the area surrounding the mansion which was the real core of the property, and the various lodges – Berkhamsted Lodge, Nettleden Lodge, Tudor Lodge, Ringshall Lodge and Thunderdell Lodge – stood as sentinels at the entrances to this inner kingdom.

The Chiltern valleys, and the lands in the vale below the hills, were prime wheat and barley growing country, and the grain produced had to be processed. One of the most interesting buildings now owned by the National Trust is Pitstone Windmill (3), perhaps the oldest of its kind in Britain, dating back at least to 1627. Like other early windmills it is a 'post mill', in which the whole wooden body of the mill, including the stones, could be turned on a large post to face the wind. It is a stunning piece of engineering, still with its traditional framework sails, across which the miller would carefully adjust the canvas to allow for wind conditions. The mill operated until 1902 when it was damaged by a storm. It was acquired by the Trust in 1937 and restored in 1963 by a group of volunteers, the leader of which subsequently donated the field in which the mill stands to the National Trust.

Below Pitstone Windmill

ROMAN INFLUENCE [AD 43–410]

With the arrival of the Romans, farming intensified, probably as bigger markets developed, but generally native farming practices continued much as before. Among the reasons the Romans were interested in Britain were its agricultural productivity and fairly complex forms of social organization. The landscape at Ashridge was probably divided amongst several farms or villas.

THE MIDDLE AGES

The land continued to be used for and shaped by agriculture ar drovers passing through Ashridge moving livestock between grazing areas and markets.

An Augustinian order, the Bonhommes, was founded here i the 13th century. They led simple lives studying, praying, tendin the sick and built an enclosed garden for growing their own foo

BRONZE AGE [from 2,300 BC]

The introduction of farming, when people learned how to produce rather than hunt and gather their food, was one of the biggest changes in human history and sees the beginning of man's shaping the world about him. The earliest surviving signs of human occupation at Ashridge are in earthworks including burial mounds or barrows.

IRON AGE [from 700 BC]

By the Iron Age much of the land across the south of Britain was under the plough and producing a large range of crops very efficiently. The hillfort on Ivinghoe Beacon was a meeting place, a market and a corral for livestock. It was close to the Icknield Way, a long-distance trading route from Wessex to East Anglia. Trees on the hills would have been cleared for livestock grazing.

THE CHALK GRASSLANDS

Chalk hills extend over the northern part of the estate, from Ivinghoe Beacon (1) to Incombe Hole (2). There are magnificent views across the countryside to the north, and towards Pitstone Windmill (3).

The open grassland in the north of the estate, on the chalk slopes of the Ivinghoe and Pitstone Hills, contrasts strongly with the wooded landscape of the clay plateau. The escarpment slopes are steep and dramatic, especially the narrow dry valley, or combe, called Incombe Hole. This was created during the last glaciation, when the area was tundra with permanently frozen subsoil. Extreme cold shattered the surface of the chalk: summer thaws made this rubble debris flow downhill, scoring this and other deep scars in the hillside.

Cultivation came to an end, especially on the steeper slopes, at the close of the Roman period and the thin, well-drained chalk soils were then grazed continuously by sheep for many centuries. The flocks were traditionally valued not only for their wool and meat, but also for the manure they produced. They were used by local farmers, in effect, as mobile muck-spreaders: grazed by day on the hills, and at night brought down to the arable fields on the lower ground. Here they were closely penned up in folds made of hazel hurdles and dunged the ground, providing fertility for the soil.

Shaping the land

Sheep were not the only stock grazed here. Rabbits are not indigenous to Britain but were introduced shortly after the Norman Conquest and were, to begin with, semi-domesticated animals, kept in special warrens which were usually located on well-drained soils. Vulnerable to predators and the elements, they might shelter beneath masses of vegetation, but were sometimes provided with artificial burrows beneath low mounds. A warren was established, perhaps in the 16th century, on the slopes just to the south-east of Ivinghoe Beacon. The area was described as 'Box Warren' in a document of 1656 and a number of outgrown strips of box, around 15 metres wide, still survive here. The strips are shown, much as

Below

Strips of box used to shelter rabbits in Box Warren

they are today, on an estate map of 1762.

Regular grazing on thin chalk soils by sheep and rabbits produces a characteristic vegetation of close-cropped turf, mainly composed of the grass called sheep's fescue, but accompanied by a wide range of wildflowers. This distinctive sward can still be found in many places on the hills but much was lost in the course of the 20th century due to changes in the ways in which the land was used.

Renewed efforts

The intensity with which the pastures were grazed declined as meat prices fell during the period of the agricultural depression, and as farmers increasingly used artificial chemicals, rather than the dung from sheep, to fertilise their fields. Coarser grasses, especially brome grass, took over and hawthorn, which had previously been kept in check by the sheep, began to increase significantly. Rabbits also increased in number, as they tended to do everywhere in England at this time, and this to some extent retarded the regeneration of scrub. But the population declined dramatically with the onset of myxomatosis in 1953, allowing hawthorn, and to some extent box and juniper, to thrive.

The National Trust began scrub clearance in the 1960s, but efforts began in earnest in the 1980s, and in 1994 sheep grazing was reintroduced with excellent results. Much of the traditional vegetation has returned, and the area is now of national or international scientific significance, one of the largest areas of chalk grassland surviving in the Chiltern Hills. But constant efforts still need to be made to keep the steeper slopes, in particular, clear of scrub.

Left Sheep on Pitstone Hill

FLORA, FAUNA AND FORTS

Rare survivors

The range of species which can be found in the area is particularly large due to the variety of the local topography, which features, unusually for the Chilterns, warm south-facing as well as cooler north-facing slopes. Such nationally rare species as the beautiful Pasque flower and the field fleawort thrive here, together with early gentian, yellow wort and an abundance of orchids such as the fragrant, pyramidal and bee orchid. The area is also of high conservation value for its invertebrates, which includes such scarce butterfly species as the Duke of Burgundy and the marbled white. The mosaic of scrub and open grassland supports a wide range of breeding birds, including meadow pipit and several species of warbler. In spring and autumn many other birds pass through on migration, including ring ouzel and wheatear, and red kite can frequently be seen wheeling overhead. Unimproved, long-established chalk grassland was once a common environment in England, but is now rare: the Ivinghoe and Pitstone Hills are vital survivors.

Ancestral traces

The use of the land for grazing, rather than as arable, in medieval and later times has also helped to preserve a wealth of ancient earthworks, which would elsewhere have been ploughed flat long ago. The most striking are to be found on Beacon Hill. At least ten barrows of Bronze Age date form a line along the ridge. They were carefully positioned so that they would be visible from the vale below, and were presumably the burial places of important local people. The most noticeable prehistoric monument, however, is Ivinghoe Beacon, a hill fort comprising a rampart and ditch. The ditch is now largely filled, and the rampart much eroded, but the site is still evocative. Excavations carried out in the 1960s revealed that the ramparts – originally a double line on the more vulnerable south-eastern side – were carefully constructed, with fences formed of close-set posts front and back, and the space between filled with chalk rubble

Below The Duke of Burgundy fritillary (*Hamearis lucina*)

The fort is an early example of its type: it was probably erected at the very end of the Bronze Age, in the middle of the 8th century BC. Although such monuments are described as forts there is much debate amongst archaeologists over their true function, with many now emphasising their role as ceremonial centres rather than simply as fortifications or defended settlements. Certainly, the careful choice of site – on a prominent, distinctively shaped hill, visible for many miles – perhaps hints at some kind of ceremonial function.

Timeless views

The hills are a wonderful place, even for those who have little knowledge of or interest in rare plants and insects, geology, or ancient monuments. They provide a sense of freedom and openness, with wide skies and extensive panoramas over the low-lying vale to the north. On a clear day it is possible to see the Berkshire Downs, many kilometres away.

Right Red kite (*Milvus milvus*)
Below Pyramidal orchids (*Anacamptis pyramidalis*) on the south-western edge of the Ivinghoe Hills

THE WOODS

Woodland of various kinds now occupies most of Ashridge, extending from Dockey Wood (4) in the north – with its magnificent displays of bluebells – to the ancient pollards of Frithsden Beeches (14) in the south.

Above Bluebells under the beech and oak trees of Dockey Wood

It is the great woods of Ashridge that most impress the visitor. They extend across 1,200 hectares (2,965 acres), making them one of the largest areas of deciduous woodland in England. In early medieval times the entire area of the clay-with-flints plateau was probably occupied by woodland, some of which had never been cleared, some of which had regenerated over abandoned Roman fields. Much was exploited as common land and so became more open in character, although never entirely losing its tree cover, and, as the intensity of grazing declined in the course of the 20th century, trees gradually returned, so that much of the woodland seen today is comparatively modern. Some of the estate woodland is ancient, however, and represents areas which were enclosed and preserved during the Middle Ages.

Maintaining standards
Most of these private woods were managed as 'coppice-with-standards', the majority of trees being cut down to their base or 'stool' at intervals of around a decade in order to produce a regular crop of straight poles suitable for fuel, fencing and a host of other uses. Only a minority of trees were allowed to grow to maturity, as 'standards', to provide larger

Tree terminology

Pollarding is done to encourage the lateral growth of branches by cutting off minor branches two or three metres above ground level, keeping the foliage out of reach of grazing animals. The tree is then allowed to regrow after the initial cutting, but once begun, pollarding requires regular maintenance by pruning. This will eventually result in a swollen top to the tree trunk with multiple new side and top shoots growing from it.

Coppicing is a traditional method of woodland management in which young tree stems are repeatedly cut down to near ground level. In subsequent growth years, many new shoots will emerge, and, after a number of years the coppiced tree, or stool, is ready to be harvested and the cycle begins again.

timbers. The coppice stools would be damaged – or even killed off entirely – if animals were allowed to graze them after they had been cut, and so they were enclosed within banks, ditches and hedges. Traces of these old enclosing banks, which show the boundaries between private property and common land, can still be found in a number of places. A few examples of ancient outgrown stools – of hornbeam, hazel, or sweet chestnut – can also still be seen but they are rare survivors, for the management of the woods has undergone a number of dramatic changes over the last three centuries.

Firstly, during the 18th century the owners of the estate began to encourage the growth of standard trees at the expense of coppice. Single stems were selected from stools and allowed to develop to maturity, while seedlings which had established themselves naturally on the woodland floor were allowed to grow uncut, in what is sometimes called the 'selection system' of forestry. Gradually, this increase in tall trees shaded out the coppice stools and killed them off, converting coppiced woodland into woods entirely composed of standard trees.

Next, in the course of the 19th century, modern forestry practices were introduced. Some areas of woodland were felled and replanted to produce stands of trees which were all of the same age, and which could all be felled and replaced together when they reached maturity, although they might on occasions be retained because of the beauty they lent to the landscape. Such plantations often contained a range of species, including fast-growing conifer 'nurses' intended to protect the young hardwoods, so that Thunderdell, for example, includes oak, chestnut and beech.

Finally, in the 20th century, it became fashionable to use conifers rather than deciduous trees for such plantations, and several areas of such relatively recent, and (for the most part) botanically uninteresting, woodland can be found on the estate.

Above left One of the large tree trunks at Frithsden Beeches bearing the signs of past pollarding

MAJESTIC OAKS AND HUMBLE FUNGI

Towering trunks

All these developments greatly altered the character of the Ashridge woods. Mature beech and oak trees are now their most striking feature but, before these changes, beech in particular would have been less dominant. Beech was especially favoured by 18th-century foresters because its seedlings are shade tolerant and thus particularly well suited to management under the selection system (see previous page). But the deep shade cast by mature beech trees also tends to suppress the growth of other species. Beech was actively encouraged not only because it made good firewood, which could be sold locally and as far afield as London, but also because it was in demand by the local furniture and wood-turning industry. The increased mechanisation of furniture production in the middle and later decades of the 19th century, especially in the town of High Wycombe, and the development of mechanised sawmills and factories allowed the use of larger timber, and so further encouraged the growth of large standard trees and discouraged coppicing. As a result of all this, mixed woodlands managed as coppice-with-standards were replaced by the majestic woods of mature oak and beech trees which are such a feature of the estate today.

Ground dwellers

All this said, few of the local woods are composed entirely of beech and oak. On the steep slopes, where the ground falls towards Aldbury, beech is accompanied by ash and some whitebeam; while on the clay-with-flints of the plateau, oak and beech are usually accompanied by ash, hornbeam and wild cherry, with sporadic examples of sweet chestnut, together with some birch and hazel. As well as being visually stunning, the woods are of immense biological interest. The oldest woods carry a rich ground flora featuring bluebell, primrose, yellow archangel and dog's mercury, with sorrel and green hellebore on the more acidic soils. The display of bluebells in Dockey Wood (4) has to be seen to be

Left Oaks in Thunderdell Wood

Opposite, top left Bluebells (*Hyacinthoides non-scripta*), wild garlic (*Allium ursinum*) and yellow archangel (*Lamiastrum galeobdolon*)

...elieved. Fungi abound, including the spectacular (but highly poisonous) fly agaric. Insect life is diverse and abundant, with good populations of many butterfly species, including speckled wood, purple hairstreak, and gatekeeper, while a wide range of woodland birds can be seen, such as hawfinch, wood warbler, and tree pipit. The larger animals are shy and retiring, and less easily seen by the visitor, but include fallow and muntjac deer, several species of bat, fox and the edible dormouse. The Ashridge woodlands also support a large population of fallow deer. These need to be managed to minimise damage to the woodland habitat and to neighbouring farmland.

Right The cap of the fly agaric (*Amonita muscaria*) is decorated with pure white, warty remnants readily washed off by rain

THE COMMONS

Much of the Ashridge Estate comprises commonland, sometimes still largely open ground, like parts of Northchurch Common (13), but nowadays usually more wooded, as at Frithsden Beeches (14).

Traditionally, a common was not an area which was owned or used by everybody. Commons had owners, usually the lord of the manor in which they lay, and they were used by defined groups of people – the commoners – for grazing livestock and in a variety of other ways. In the early Middle Ages the area around Ashridge was probably one vast tract of upland common, exploited by people living in the surrounding villages, but by late medieval times this had been divided up between different communities, so that Pitstone, Ivinghoe, Aldbury, Northchurch and Berkhamsted all came to have their own defined areas of common land.

Below Greetings from Berkhamsted Common

11. BERKHAMPSTEAD. THE COMMON

Commons usage

The commons were probably originally wooded, but by the Middle Ages grazing pressure had produced a mosaic of grassland, heath and wood pasture – that is, areas of open woodland in which animals were grazed and in which most of the trees were pollarded rather than coppiced. The commons were also cut for a variety of other materials. Gorse was harvested for fuel, which was used both domestically and in local kilns, and heather and bracken for animal bedding.

Reclaiming the commons

Regular cutting and grazing prevented the regeneration of scrub and woodland, creating and preserving extensive open swathes of heather and gorse. But from the late 19th century these traditional uses declined, and grazing more or less ceased in the 1920s. The Commons Registration Act 1965 is still very much in force, protecting the rights of registered individuals to cut wood and gather bracken, but these rights are these days little exercised. As a result, formerly open grass and heath have been colonised by hawthorn scrub and by birch and oak, leading in places to the development of oak-birch woodland, or woodland dominated by ash. Only small fragments of acid grassland and heathland vegetation survive, usually beside the main

ides, although the Trust is actively engaged in increasing their area.

Natural history

This radical change in the appearance of the landscape – a clear indication of the extent to which, far from being natural, the local environment has been shaped by centuries of use and management – has led to the decline in many important species. But much of interest remains on the commons. Of particular importance are the ancient oak and beech pollards which can still be found in a number of places, often buried within much later scrub and woodland. In the area known as Frithsden Beeches (14) there is a remarkable collection of around a hundred ancient beech pollards, which forms one of the most important examples of a beech wood pasture surviving in England. These ancient trees, as well as being living connections with the remote past, are a particularly important habitat for a range of rare insects, bats, fungi and lichens. But the surrounding scrub and grassland are also home to a wide range of wildlife, as are the various ponds which were originally dug to provide water for the livestock grazed on the commons.

Furthermore, the fact that the commons have not been ploughed for centuries has ensured that they contain a treasure trove of archaeological features in addition to the wealth of Ashridge's natural history.

Above The Frithsden beech trees support a huge diversity of animal life

CHANGING TIMES

For hundred of years the landscape of Ashridge had been shaped by farming and the leisure activities of the rich. But from the later 19th century, reflecting the rapidly changing face of English society, Ashridge was the scene of dramatic and permanent changes.

In the second half of the 19th century the commons of the Ashridge Estate were increasingly used for recreation, especially by people living in Berkhamsted. But in 1865 the 2nd Earl Brownlow enclosed around a third of Berkhamsted Common with five-feet high iron fences. It was an illegal act, as he had bought out most, but not all, of the commoners. One of those that did not sell was Augustus Smith, a wealthy Berkhamsted resident (and Lord of the Scilly Isles). On the night of 7 March 1866 he brought 120 labourers by train from London to break down the fence. In the subsequent court case, in which the newly formed Commons Preservation Society was much involved, the Earl was defeated and the commons saved, for now.

Right The front cover of Thomas Place's proposal for Ashridge

Selling up

During the 20th century, and especially in the interwar years, many large estates were broken up. Agriculture was relatively unprofitable after the 1870s due to the scale of foreign imports, and the rents which landowners received from farms suffered. Changes in the organisation of local and national government ensured that great families were less involved in politics, and therefore felt it less necessary to display their wealth by maintaining large estates. On top of this, a marked increase in death duties from 1909 ensured that landed families were often obliged to sell up following the death of an owner.

The threat of Metroland

The 3rd Earl Brownlow decided to get rid of all his lands in southern England to concentrate resources on his Lincolnshire estates. On his death, his will stated that Ashridge be sold to save Belton. This was a time when, with improvements in transport, large areas of the Chiltern Hills were being suburbanised – transformed into what John Betjeman described as 'Metroland'. There was a real danger that significant portions of Ashridge would be built on. Residents were concerned and a number, including the historian G.M.Trevelyan, urged the National Trust (then only a quarter of a century old) to purchase what they could of the estate. A fund-raising campaign was launched locally – but gained national support – and schoolchildren were asked to save 'pennies for Ashridge'.

New owners

The campaign was successful, and in 1926 around 1,700 acres were acquired. The following year the remainder of the estate was bought by Thomas Place, a property speculator who set about trying to build a golf course with housing around the fairways. The golf course was built but the housing was not. To prevent further development, the Trust acquired more parcels of land, so that by 1930 they owned around 4,000 acres of the former estate.

The mansion and its gardens were purchased in 1928 by Urban Broughton, who gave them to the Conservative Party to be used as a college for political and economic studies – named the Bonar Law College after Andrew Bonar Law, Prime Minister in 1922–23. In 1959 the mansion became the Ashridge Management College, now known as the Ashridge Business School. A large part of the north park became the Ashridge Golf Club, opened in 1932. But, thanks to the efforts of local campaigners and the involvement of the National Trust, the woods and the commons of Ashridge had again been saved.

URGENT APPEAL TO THE PUBLIC.

THREE WEEKS FOR DECISION.
TO THE EDITOR OF THE TIMES.

Sir,—We desire to express our strong sympathy with the proposal to acquire as much as possible of Ashridge Park and the adjoining woods and downland to be held by the National Trust for the benefit of the public. We understand that the National Trust has already at its disposal for this purpose a sum of £20,000, contributed by an anonymous donor. Negotiations have been on foot for the purchase with this sum of a stretch of land between Ivinghoe Beacon and Berkhamsted Common. We hope that there will be no doubt that the Trustees will consent to the carrying through of these negotiations to a successful conclusion.

But we wish to express a hope that much more than this may be done. We believe that there are few, if any, parks that combine so many features of desirability for public acquisition as Ashridge. It is within easy reach of London, and has within the last few years come to be visited by a very large number of persons on week-ends and holidays ; it is amongst the most richly timbered of parks, and it has adjoining it stretches of downland, with magnificent views.

For all these reasons we earnestly hope that the Trustees will see their way to give further time for the raising of money. In that case we have little doubt that the generous example set by the anonymous donor will find many imitators, and that, with the support of those who care for the preservation of the kind of woodland scenery in which England stands unrivalled, a very much larger area of this beautiful country than has so far been contemplated may be secured for the permanent enjoyment of the nation.

It is understood that the Trustees stipulate that they should have some idea of the area to be acquired for the public, and the sum that is likely to be raised at the expiration of three weeks from now.

The time, therefore, available for raising the money is very short ; we trust that the general public will realize that the more generous the response to this appeal, the greater will be the area of the property secured for the public benefit.

Contributions should be sent to the Secretary of the National Trust, at 7, Buckingham Palace-gardens, S.W.1. Cheques should be made payable to " The National Trust." and crossed " National Provincial Bank of England."

Yours faithfully,
STANLEY BALDWIN.
J. RAMSAY MAC DONALD.
OXFORD AND ASQUITH.
GREY OF FALLODON (Vice-President of the National Trust).
The National Trust. 7, Buckingham Palace-gardens, S.W.1, Oct. 19.

Left Letter to the editor from the serving and two former Prime Ministers: Stanley Baldwin (1923–24, 1924–29, 1935–37), J. Ramsay MacDonald (1924, 1929–31, 1931–35) and H.H. Asquith (1908–16); *The Times*, 20 Oct 1925

ASHRIDGE AT WAR

Just as the natural beauty and recreational opportunities of Ashridge were attracting more and more visitors from far and wide, another invasion saw areas of the estate commandeered for rather different reasons.

Managing a landscape as extensive and diverse as that of the Ashridge Estate was no easy matter, especially one so close to the expanding suburbs of north-west London. By the time the Trust acquired the property in 1926, car ownership was increasing rapidly, and in the inter-war years pressure from cars and motorcycles caused considerable problems, with people often driving far across the unfenced commons to find a suitable site for a picnic. In dealing with this problem the Trust were helped by changes in the law – the passing of the Traffic Act of 1931 – which made it easy to prevent cars from trespassing more

than fifteen yards from a public road. From this time, too, discreet barriers were created at critical entry points, and other minor restrictions imposed to ensure that visitors could enjoy the peace of the countryside undisturbed.

Military occupation

That peace was, however, shattered by the outbreak of the Second World War in 1939. The woodland and scrub of the estate provided an excellent military training ground, and a number of army camps were erected here, occupied by the 5th Highland Division, the

Below The XIth Hussars officers were stationed at Ashridge

XIth Hussars and American, Dutch and Polish troops. There were also observation posts manned by the Royal Observer Corps, while Ashridge House itself became an emergency hospital. Much timber was cut out of the local woods to meet the critical war-time shortages. This phase of history has, like those before it, left its traces on the landscape. The remains of practice trenches can, for example, still be found in Thunderdell Wood (near (7) on map); while the drive from the B4506 to the Bridgewater Monument – which follows the line of the old Princes Riding – was surfaced by Belgian troops. Half way along an open rectangular area used as a parade ground, still known as Barracks Square, there are traces of old Nissen huts (not far from (6)).

Right Eisenhower inspecting the troops on the parade ground

Below Hospital huts photographed in the 1960s, shortly before they were demolished

LANDSCAPE IN TRUST

An ancient landscape bearing the signs of countless generations is now held in trust for ever and for everyone. It is hoped that, through the care of the National Trust and its staff, Ashridge will continue to reveal more stories of its long past whilst continuing to delight future visitors with its wide open spaces and far-reaching views.

Since the Second World War, the number of visitors has continued to grow, as the surrounding areas of Hertfordshire and Buckinghamshire have themselves become more and more crowded with houses and people. Today the estate receives more than 500,000 visitors a year, and the National Trust has a careful balancing act to maintain. It has a duty to preserve the rich historical and natural heritage it holds in trust, and the rural tranquillity which people come from far and wide to enjoy. Yet it must do so without imposing too many restrictions on visitors, who seek that feeling of freedom which extensive tracts of wild and open country provide, and who do not want to see this spoilt by signs and barriers. Above all, this apparently natural landscape needs constant and rigorous management, including such things as the removal of scrub to allow species-rich grassland to flourish. To carry out this vital work, the estate, self-financing since 1926, liaises regularly with other local landowners and enjoys the support of volunteers, especially the Friends of Ashridge. Only with active, careful management can this precious landscape can be preserved for future generations.

Below Volunteers and staff are crucial in preserving this landscape for ever and for everyone